Philip Ardagh's Shortcuts

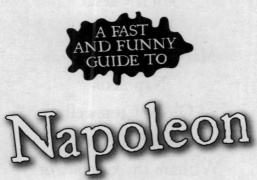

A FAST
AND FUNNY
GUIDE TO

Napoleon

Philip Ardagh's Shortcuts

Philip Ardagh's Shortcuts

A FAST
AND FUNNY
GUIDE TO

Napoleon

Illustrated by Mike Phillips

MACMILLAN CHILDREN'S BOOKS

For Henry Todd.
Watch out for the wallpaper!

First published 2000 by Macmillan Children's Books

This edition published 2013 by Macmillan Children's Books
a division of Macmillan Publishers Limited
20 New Wharf Road, London N1 9RR
Basingstoke and Oxford
Associated companies throughout the world
www.panmacmillan.com

ISBN 978-1-4472-4023-5

Text copyright © Philip Ardagh 2000
Illustrations copyright © Mike Phillips 2000

1 3 5 7 9 8 6 4 2

A CIP catalogue record for this book is available from the British Library.

Printed and bound by CPI Group (UK) Ltd, Croydon CR0 4YY

CONTENTS

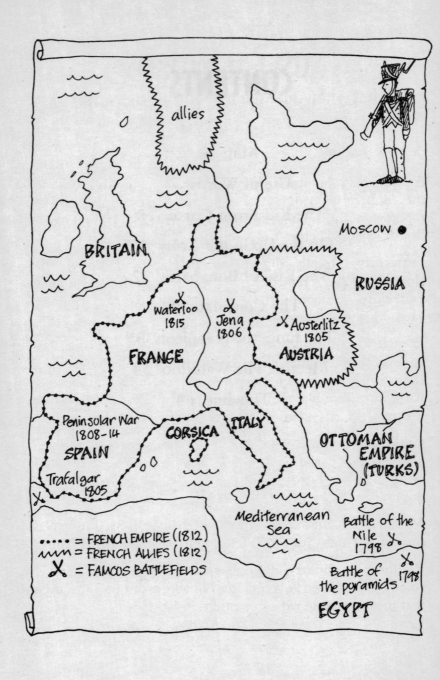

USEFUL WORDS
(but, then again, most words are useful, aren't they?)

Aristocrat A member of the aristocracy or nobility. One of the 'upper' or 'ruling' classes. French aristocrats had a reputation for being cruel or unthinking to the French 'lower' classes, before the revolution.

Fraternity Literally, this means 'brotherhood' but in the slogan of the French Revolution – 'Liberty! Equality! Fraternity!' – it applied to women too. It meant treating each other like a brother or sister.

French Revolution Starting in 1789, this was an uprising against the monarchy, resulting in the execution of King Louis XVI and Queen Marie Antoinette at the guillotine. After the Republic was created over 14,000 people were executed as its 'enemies' – including many revolutionaries!

Guillotine A large, wooden-framed machine with a sharp blade, which could be dropped on a person's neck to chop off his or her head. This method of execution was very popular in the French Revolution.

Monarchy A monarchy is a country, nation or state ruled over by a king or queen. The monarchy is the royal family.

Republic A country, nation or state – yes, them again – ruled by an elected government, not a king or queen . . . even if it means getting rid of one first.

THE KID FROM CORSICA

Napoleon, possibly the most famous Frenchman the world has ever known, wasn't – er – actually French. His father's name was Carlo Buonaparte and his mother's maiden name was Letizia Ramolino . . . neither of which sound as French as *café au lait*. They were a Corsican family; Corsica being a Mediterranean island off Italy. The Corsicans wanted to rule the island for themselves but were governed by the Genoese (from Genoa, which was then an independent city state in Italy). Napoleon's father was a strong supporter of the Corsican independence leader, Paoli.

ALL CHANGE

Then two great events occurred in 1769. One had an immediate effect: the Genoese had sold the island to the French as part of a treaty in 1768, and the French now invaded. The second was the birth of Napoleon on 15 August. Napoleon's father, Carlo, got along a lot better with the French than he ever had with the Genoese. In fact, he soon had an important job with the French administration on the island. One person of Genoese origin that Carlo *did* get along with, though, was his wife Letizia.

A BIG BROOD

Napoleon was to be one of eight children. First came big brother Joseph (whom Napoleon probably bullied as a boy), then Napoleon himself, followed by Lucien (who's pretty important later on), Maria (who later changed her name to Elisa), Louis (his favourite brother), Pauline (said to be stunningly beautiful), Caroline and, last but not least, Jèrôme (the only one with funny accents). Their mother was said to be very beautiful too, but poorly educated. She loved her children deeply but was always penny-pinching, which you probably would be too if you had such a large family to look after.

THE BIGGER THE BROTHER, THE HARDER THEY BAWL!

SCHOLARSHIP BOYS

Carlo Buonaparte became more and more important on the island, and a good friend of the French governor of Corsica, a man named de Marbeuf. It was de Marbeuf who managed to arrange for the oldest Buonaparte boy, Joseph, to get nominated for a scholarship to the College of Autun. He also arranged for the young Napoleon to be nominated for a scholarship to the Military Academy at Brienne. Both schools were in France, and the boys had to learn to speak French first. (These were royal schools because, back then, France was still ruled by a king.)

STICKING OUT, LIKE A NOSE!

Napoleon spent three months, aged nine, at school in Autun before going to Brienne. He seems to have seen himself as a Corsican being taught amongst the French conquerors, so didn't fit in and was unpopular with the other kids. It was at Autun that he got the nickname 'Paille-au-nez-Napollione' which, I'm reliably informed by a brainy person who can actually read French, means 'Straw-nose-Napoleon'. Perhaps this was because, like a nose, he stuck out! (He later earned the nickname of the 'Little Corporal'. Fully grown he was only 5 feet 2 inches – that's less than 158cm – tall.) At Brienne, rather than being one of the crowd, he had a few close friends. He's supposed to have been mad keen on history and brilliant at maths.

RISING THROUGH THE RANKS

After his years at the Military Academy at Brienne, the young Napoleon was selected to be sent to the army cadet school in Paris. Though the building itself was grand and the furnishing plush and comfortable, the day-to-day routine for cadets was both physically and mentally tough. In his final exams, to get him into the French artillery corps, Napoleon did so well in maths that he was immediately commissioned as a second lieutenant. (Most cadets had to work their way through other stages before reaching such dizzy heights. No wonder most of them hated him!)

FIRST POSTING, FIRST GIRLFRIEND

In 1785, aged sixteen, Lieutenant Napoleon Buonaparte joined the 'Regiment of the Father' – 'the father' being the king, I suppose – which was stationed at a place called Valence in the Rhône Valley. This was where he met his first girlfriend, Caroline de Colombier. Although he wrote to her regularly in later life, even after she married, perhaps to call Caroline his girlfriend is a bit of an exaggeration. By Napoleon's own admission, all they did was eat cherries together. (Yup, you read that right: eat cherries together.) But he was obviously very fond of her!

HOME & AWAY

1785 was also the year that Napoleon's father, Carlo, died. From 1786 to 1788, Napoleon's regiment was posted to a place called Auxonne, but he was very rarely there. He was an officer in the old royal army of France, and it was ridiculously easy for him to get leave. He spent most of that time in Paris or back home in Corsica – the first time he'd been back home in eight years. (He'd always sent money home though, even though his soldier's pay was poor. He knew his mother needed every penny he could spare.)

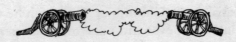

THE FRENCH REVOLUTION

1789 was the year of the French Revolution, in which the monarchy and aristocracy was thrown aside (with many people being beheaded at the guillotine) and 'the people' seized power . . . The revolutionaries' slogan was: 'Liberty! Equality! Fraternity!' France now became a republic. (1789 was also the year that Napoleon nearly drowned!)

THE PLACE OF THE ARMY

Instead of being loyal to the King, most ordinary soldiers were loyal to the people. They remained in the army but were now there to defend the republic rather than the monarchy. Most of the senior officers, from aristocratic (pro-royal) families, however, deserted their posts, but middle-ranking officers, such as Napoleon, stayed put. As a Corsican, Napoleon thought that the French Revolution might, in the end, lead to independence for his island home.

A WIND OF CHANGE

In September 1789, Napoleon went home to Corsica and, against the wishes of the authorities, helped to set up a National Citizens Guard to defend his beloved island. Then, in November, an assembly in Paris announced that Corsica was no longer a colony of France but a part of it. Corsicans would, therefore, become French men and women, with the same rights and freedoms. Even the independence leader, Paoli, was allowed to return to Corsica and head its army. Although Napoleon would've liked to have seen a totally independent Corsica, he could see the fairness of what the

French had done. Over time, he became more and more loyal to France, the 'mother country'. In other words, he began to feel French.

BY HOOK OR BY CROOK

In 1791, at a time when the army was reorganized following the revolution, Napoleon was promoted to first lieutenant. (The Regiment of the Father was now renamed 'The First Regiment'.) He joined the Regiment of Grenoble, then stationed at Valance . . . but it wasn't long before he was back on leave. Then he somehow managed to wangle three months' attachment to a volunteer Corsican battalion. He was supposed to be back with his regular regiment by 1 April 1792, but he chose to ignore the order.

ANOTHER REVOLUTION

Riots broke out in the Corsican city of Ajaccio (where Napoleon had been born) on Easter Sunday 1792.

14

Napoleon's volunteer forces were so ruthless in putting down the riots, using much more force than necessary and being downright violent for the sake of it, that he was denounced by many to the Corsican deputies in Paris. There were even complaints about Napoleon's tactics made in the Legislative Assembly. It was time for Napoleon to head back to France . . .

PROBLEMS IN PARIS

Napoleon returned to Paris on 28 May 1792. By 10 July, the Minister of War had reinstated him to the regular army, but now with the rank of captain . . . but still he went back to Corsica! This time it was because he had to accompany his sister, Elisa, home. Then, in October, the French decided to invade the island of Sardinia from Corsica. Thousands of troops were sent over to Corsica from Marseilles to fight alongside the Corsicans.

INTO THE JAWS OF DEFEAT

While the French attacked the Sardinian capital, Cagliari, Napoleon led his battalion of Corsican volunteers to the Sardinian island of Maddalena, in January 1793. Everything seemed to be going his way, and it wouldn't be long until the harbour and port surrendered . . . except that a number of the volunteers suddenly panicked, for some reason, and mutinied against the officers! The attack force collapsed and had to make an undignified retreat. 1793 also saw the execution of King Louis XVI, and Britain declaring war on France. The Corsican leader, Paoli, and his supporter, Pozzo di Borgo, were seen by many Frenchmen as being too pro-British for comfort. At the start of 1793, Saliceti was sent to take control of Corsican forces from him.

CIVIL WAR

Soon, civil war broke out. Paoli and his supporters held half the island, including Ajaccio. Supporting the other side, Napoleon fought against him and, having failed to take the citadel off him, almost ended up Paoli's prisoner. Fortunately Napoleon managed to get away and join forces with Saliceti (a commissioner of France's Army of Italy) at the northern Corsican town of Bastia. The rest of the Buonaparte family were forced to flee the island, to live in exile. Their homes were pillaged (which is a brilliant word, meaning robbed, usually during war). Napoleon, meanwhile, was still trying to whip up support in Ajaccio but, having failed, went with his family to France.

ON THE UP IN THE ARMY

All was not well back on the French mainland either. Many provinces, particularly those in the south, had risen up against the revolutionary authorities in Paris. In other words, the king and aristocracy might have got the chop, but that didn't stop the revolutionaries fighting amongst themselves. Napoleon found himself rising swiftly through the ranks. Loyal to the leaders in Paris, he took part in the siege of the town of Toulon, where he really made a name for himself. Promoted to lieutenant colonel, he caught the eye of the Revolution's leader, Robespierre, was labelled a 'reliable patriot' and promoted yet again, this time to brigadier general.

A CHANGE OF FORTUNE

Napoleon worked alongside Robespierre's brother, Augustin, and his name was soon linked with the Robespierres, which was all fine and dandy so long as Robespierre was in power. In 1794, Robespierre lost power (and was eventually guillotined, which makes sense of that old saying 'those who live by the sword die by the sword' though, in this case, it was a much bigger blade). From being up-there-with-the-big-names, Napoleon was now in a very dangerous position. He was arrested and accused of having carried out acts of treason against France.

UPS AND DOWNS

Fortunately for Napoleon, an inquiry cleared him and he was set free after a matter of days. He found himself posted to France's 'Army of Italy' – in those days, Italy wasn't a single, independent country but was made up of independent city states such as Genoa – and planned the battle of Dego, which became a French victory. In 1795, Napoleon was given the task of trying to recapture Corsica, but this failed. Corsicans were now seen as allies of the British (because of Paoli's British sympathies), and Napoleon was seen by some of the Revolution's new leaders as a Corsican . . . so he was hurriedly reassigned to the 'Army of the West', which was fighting the Wars of the Vendée. These were a series of pro-royalist peasant uprisings in the Pays-de-la-Loire region of France, with Frenchmen (and women) fighting Frenchmen (and women).

GETTING OUT OF IT

Napoleon got out of going by pretending to be ill! Then, as luck would have it, a member of the Committee of Public

Safety called Pontècoulant appointed him Head of the Committee's Topographical Bureau. (Topography, in this case, was to do with military planning and maps.) Napoleon then decided he wanted to lead a mission to Turkey, and Pontècoulant backed him, but then the Ministry of War told him that he was no longer a general because he'd failed to join the Army of the West.

REVOLUTION FROM WITHIN

These were tough times in revolutionary France, with different groups forever turning against each other. The government suddenly found itself faced by 25,000 unfriendly troops, whilst it could only raise 5,000. Napoleon's reputation as a good soldier was well-known, so the past was forgotten and he was hurriedly called in to help. He successfully saved the government against the attack on its buildings and was promoted to major general. Soon after that, he became the commander-in-chief of the 'Army of the Interior', with a huge salary of 48,000 francs and control of the police and secret service. (The first thing he did was to move his mother and family into a bigger and better house in the swanky part of town.)

WHEN THOUGHTS TURN TO LOVE

Now that Napoleon was such an important and famous man, he turned his attention to getting married to a certain Josephine de Beauharnais – who wasn't his first choice for a wife, by the way. (In fact, he was still engaged to someone else when he was about to marry her!) Josephine, whose triple-barrelled first name was really Marie-Joséphe-Rose, came from a rich aristocratic family and was the young widow of the equally rich Vicomte de Beauharnais. During the Revolution, he'd had his head chopped off at the guillotine – a fate which Josephine herself only narrowly avoided, leaving her and their two children alone and penniless. She soon became friends with Barras, the man who'd commanded the Army of the Interior before Napoleon, and lived in some comfort once again. When Napoleon met her, he fell head-over-heels in passionate love. They became man and wife on 9 March 1796.

THE NAME GAME

A few days before the wedding, Napoleon received yet another promotion. He was made commander-in-chief of the Army of Italy. One of the first things he did was change the spelling of his surname. Out went 'Buonaparte' with a 'u' which was, after all, originally a name from Genoa on the Italian mainland and, therefore looked Italian – and the Italians were France's enemies – and in came 'Bonaparte' which somehow looked and sounded much more French.

THE RISE OF BONAPARTE

Napoleon really proved himself as a great soldier, beyond any doubt, during what are known as his Italian Campaigns. Many battles were fought and some saw Napoleon himself in the thick of the action. Back in France, the Directory gave even more power directly to the generals. The Directory was the main seat of French Revolutionary government, with its deputies in the Council of the Ancients and the Council of the Five Hundred.

ON THE UP AND UP

By the middle of 1797, the French were back in control of Corsica and Napoleon's mother returned to the island and the family home. By the end of the year, thanks to Napoleon, much of Italy found itself under French control too. Napoleon's greatest resistance came from the Austrians, but a treaty between France and Austria – called the Campo Formio – was signed on 18 October 1797. (Napoleon also seized masses of Italian art treasures for France, as the booties of war.) Following the treaty, the Directory appointed Napoleon as the head of the 'Army of England' – England being France's favourite enemy. After attending the Congress of Rastadt, between the French and the German Empire, he returned to France in December 1797. The Directory gave Napoleon a hero's welcome but, after the official ceremonies, he took a low profile. Instead of strutting around in his famous uniform, he wore civilian clothes and steered clear of other soldiers and political leaders. Instead, he chummied up to writers and scientists and thinkers. This was a smart move. The Directory was worried that this hero-worshipped soldier might get too big for his boots . . .

MAKING PLANS

Napoleon was still doing what he did on behalf of the Directory in Paris. They were the rulers of the republic, not him . . . but it's clear that he already had his eye on being France's ruler one day. He described the members of the Directory as 'lawyers', and he didn't use the term nicely. But Napoleon was biding his time. In his own words, 'the pear was not yet ripe'.

A NEW GOAL

Napoleon studied the possibility of launching a direct attack on the British, then decided against it, even though the Directory insisted he did! He had 57 battleships and about 50,000 men but knew that the British fleet was far better organized than the French. So he turned his attention to somewhere completely different: Egypt. And you can't get more different than that. But Napoleon felt sure that, to upset and undermine the British, he must seize Egypt. Why? Because if he could control Egypt it would be a good base from which to take over India which was under the control of British traders. Well, that was his excuse anyway.

EYES ON EGYPT

So, on 23 February 1798, Napoleon tried to convince the Directory that France shouldn't attack Britain but Egypt instead. On 5 March, his plan was actually approved! He was later instructed to take Malta and Egypt and take control of the Red Sea. Napoleon's forces gathered at Toulon. After being delayed by bad weather, he finally sailed from Toulon on 19 May, with 400 ships. He not only took 38,000 troops but also 150 archaeologists, scientists, engineers and even poets and painters, to try to convince the French what a jolly important expedition this really was!

LUCK ON HIS SIDE

Once Napoleon's fleet set off from Toulon, he could have expected it to have been open to attack from Britain's fleet — led by the legendary British admiral, Lord Nelson. Could have. But luck really was on Napoleon's side. The French fleet's departure had been delayed by a terrible storm . . . a storm so terrible that it had damaged most of Lord Nelson's ships. The British fleet had to withdraw to Sardinia for some serious repair work! Not only that, the British didn't yet have any real idea where the French might be heading! On 10 June 1798, Napoleon's forces took control of the island of Malta.

A WORTHY OPPONENT

Lord Nelson was no fool and soon guessed what Napoleon was up to. He took his ships to the Egyptian port of Alexandria . . . only to find that the French weren't there. So, assuming he'd misread Napoleon's plans after all, he left. Less than two days later, the French fleet arrived. What Lord Nelson hadn't realized was that he'd simply beaten the French to it! With news of the French's arrival, Lord Nelson now returned to Egypt and, on 1 August, found the French fleet anchored in Aboukir Bay. Napoleon and his men had gone ashore to occupy the country. Lord Nelson destroyed all but two of the battleships in what became known as the Battle of the Nile. Satisfied at a job well done, and that the French expedition would soon collapse with no ships to return to, Lord Nelson left for Naples.

ALL'S WELL ON LAND

As it turned out, all was well for Napoleon on land. On 21 July, he'd fought the Battle of the Pyramids at Embabah against 6,000 cavalry and 12,000 infantry. These men were no match against Napoleon's highly trained French troops. At the time, Egypt was not ruled by the Egyptians but by Mameluke beys (Mamelukes were a military class, once Turkish slaves, and beys were their 'overlords') and it was these whom Napoleon fought. He was victorious and, when news reached him on 13 August of his fleet's destruction, he not only stayed calm but stayed put.

TURKEY TROUBLE

The Turks, who had their own claim to Egypt, declared war on France on 9 September. When news of this reached the Egyptian city of Cairo on 16 October, there was an uprising against the French occupiers. This was ruthlessly crushed. Then, in January 1799, Napoleon discovered that Syria was preparing for an attack on Egypt. On 10 February, he headed for Palestine with an army of about 13,000 men, capturing the port of Gaff, in March, along the way. This impressive military victory was tainted by the murder of 3,000 Turks – men, women and children – *after* they'd surrendered and been taken prisoners. They were killed not with bullets but with bayonets. The excuse was that this had been a 'necessary' military move because Napoleon didn't have enough men to escort them or supplies to feed them, but there's no escaping the fact that this was a terrible thing to do. (Many of Napoleon's own men, meanwhile, were now victims of the bubonic plague. As a morale-booster, he was brave enough to visit them in military hospital.)

MORE VICTORIES AT LAST

After failing to take Acre, an important city-port in the eastern Mediterranean, Napoleon returned to Cairo. His contingency of 13,000 troops had fallen to 8,000 and he now had to face an invading Turkish army of 20,000, coming across from the island of Rhodes. On 25 July, the forces faced each other at Aboukir. Through sheer brilliant generalship – if there is such a word – Napoleon's forces were victorious. Egypt was now free from any immediate military threat.

SNEAKY MOVES!

On 2 August, Napoleon discovered – from a French newspaper! – that there was renewed war in Italy (with France losing much ground), something the Directory had failed to tell him. On 24 August, he slipped out of Alexandria with a small group of men, in four small ships and in utter secrecy. His departure was so secret, in fact, that the poor guy who took over from him as commander in Egypt – one general Klèber – didn't know that he'd had the job thrust upon him until after Napoleon had gone! As it was, France's grip on Egypt soon crumbled – if there is such a thing as a crumbling grip – and she was to surrender the country to Britain.

ACCORDING TO MY HOROSCOPE, I'M GOING TO RETURN TO FRANCE AND END UP EMPEROR

'HOME' ONCE MORE

Napoleon's four ships made it past the watchful eyes of the British fleet to the French town of Frèjus on 9 October 1799. From there, he headed for Paris up the Rhône Valley and via Lyon. He was greeted with wild enthusiasm along the way and the journey became more of a triumphal procession of a returning conquering hero. But not everyone was thrilled by his return. One general went as far as suggesting to the Directory that they should court-martial Napoleon for deserting his army in Egypt. The members of the Directory were only too well aware that (whatever the truth in these accusations) Napoleon could be treated as nothing less than a hero. Public opinion was all-important to France's rulers . . . and the public seemed to love Napoleon, for the time being at least.

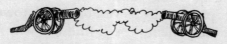

A DIRECTORY IN CHAOS

The Directory had been through many changes, but the one thing it could always pretty much be guaranteed to be was divided. Few of its members could agree on anything. It stumbled on with no clear policies or driving force. This was the centre of French government in the republic, yet it was corrupt and weak. In May 1799, a man named Sieyés became a member of the Directory and he had PLANS. He knew that, to survive, France needed strong leadership and, to get this, he'd need to stage a coup d'ètat (which is polite French for a sudden violent or illegal seizure of government). All he needed was a well-respected soldier to head the coup . . .

AN UPCOMING COUP

Napoleon finally chose to go along with Sieyés and his coup d'ètat . . . not that he was going to let Sieyés dictate what he did (but he wasn't about to admit that to Sieyés now, was he?). Sieyés's coup became known as the 'Brumaire' after the name of the second month in the new revolutionary calendar, in which it took place. (Brumaire meant 'Month of Mist' and was from 23 October to 21 November.) It went far from smoothly.

THE PLAN

Experts who understand this sort of thing say that the Brumaire wasn't really one coup d'ètat but two. The original coup, planned by Sieyés, became known as the Days of St-Cloud. (Be patient. You'll find out why in a minute.) Sieyés would invoke a special, rather quirky, clause in the Constitution which allowed a shift in the balance of power. As well as the Directory, the French parliament was made up of a number of councils. Sieyés would fix it so that the French Council of Ancients would vote for the councils to meet at St-Cloud instead of Paris, and then introduce a new constitution for France. They would shape this constitution how they wanted it, and would end up with Napoleon as a

figurehead. This wasn't to be a military coup. The fact that everyone knew that Napoleon had the army behind him should be enough to make their opponents take him seriously! That was the idea . . .

BUMBLING BEGINNINGS

On 18 Brumaire (9 November) the Council of the Ancients voted to move the councils from Paris to St-Cloud just as planned. (Most of Sieyés's opponents didn't even know that this extraordinary meeting was taking place so didn't attend and, therefore, couldn't vote against the move.) Once news got out, however, there was plenty of time for his enemies to gather and make counter-plans. Sieyés suggested mass arrests but Napoleon, knowing how this would seem to the public, told him not to bother, saying that he had no fear of such 'feeble enemies'.

BIG TROUBLE

By the next day/19 Brumaire/10 November (take your pick), things had taken a turn for the worse. Napoleon was surrounded by angry deputies who called him a dictator and tyrant and (probably) plenty more besides. Some even grabbed him by the collar and gave him a good shake, which wasn't the kind of treatment he was used to! He was eventually rescued by a detachment of grenadiers, but not before someone shouted 'Outlaw him!' (Those were the very words that had been shouted at the mighty Robespierre during his downfall . . . and we all know what happened to him.) It's largely thanks to Napoleon's brother Lucien that he survived this first part of the coup. No great fan of Napoleon, Lucien had risen through the political ranks in his own right. As president of the Council of Five Hundred, he made sure the vote to outlaw him never happened.

A HORSE! A HORSE!

Napoleon, meanwhile, had managed to get on his horse and ride up and down in front of the soldiers guarding the council. He played the injured innocent, saying that he'd come along there today to try to save the Republic, and what thanks had he got? 'Dagger blows from a minority of assassins!' (This was, of course, a whopping lie. There'd been no daggers.) Not only did this conciliar guard know what a great soldier Napoleon was, and about all the victories he'd won for France, but they also saw the blood on his face. (Little did they know that he'd probably scratched himself!) Maybe he really had been attacked? They were beginning to waver in his favour.

A MASTER STROKE

Napoleon's stroke of genius was then to have a small group of men to go and 'save' his brother Lucien from the council. When Lucien appeared, Napoleon pressed a sword against his chest, announcing that he swore an oath to kill his own brother if he ever attacked 'the liberty of the French people'. Then, unopposed by the conciliar guard, he sent a group of grenadiers – with pointy, pointy bayonets fixed to the ends of their rifles – into the Council Hall. Although he had ordered not a drop of blood to be shed, the members of the council (deputies) weren't to know that! Most fled, with many of them trying to climb out of the windows.

CONSUL POWER

At seven o'clock that evening, the Council of Ancients voted for three provisional consuls to rule France, until three could be properly elected. They were: Sieyés, his supporter Ducos, and Napoleon himself. Later that night, Napoleon's brother Lucien gathered together the remainder of the Council of Five Hundred – which, that night, should really have been called the Council of Less Than A Hundred Actually – to confirm the appointments by the Ancients. Back in Paris, Napoleon issued an official proclamation repeating the whopper about his being attacked with daggers, and announcing that the French republic was now under the rule of the Consulate.

THE CONSULATE

Sieyés, whose idea the coup had been in the first place, tried to build some safeguards into the new constitution to make sure that the First Consul – the 'head' of the three consuls – could be controlled and prevented from becoming a dictator but (surprise, surprise) Napoleon, who had his eye on that job, had different ideas. He now pulled off his coup-within-a-coup.

POLITICAL PUNCH

Just as this new constitution was about to be officially adopted and three consuls nominated – Napoleon was only one of three provisional consuls until the proper consuls were chosen, remember – he struck. Instead of a vote to see who should be put forward as consuls, Napoleon insisted that Sieyés should choose them himself . . . and, with the power and popularity he now had behind him, you didn't argue when Napoleon *insisted* on anything. So Sieyés did the choosing, but he realized that he'd have to choose the candidates Napoleon wanted him to choose! Napoleon now found himself First Consul and ruler of France.

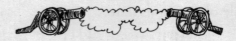

NEW POPE, NEW PLANS

Napoleon struck a deal with the Pope which finally became French law in April 1802. This 'concordat' recognized the Roman

Catholic faith as the religion of 'the majority of Frenchmen' and Roman Catholics were guaranteed freedom of worship in France, so long as they didn't break civil order rules. In return, the Pope (who had hoped the concordat would refer to Roman Catholicism as the established religion in France, but hadn't got his way) would let the First Consul nominate his own bishops. Most existing clergy would be required to resign too. All Church land confiscated by the revolution would remain state rather than Church land, but the government would now pay all clergymen's salaries.

REVOLUTIONARY REFORMS

From mid-1800 to mid-1803, a whole new infrastructure – or framework – was created for the running of France, covering everything from administration, finance, the law, the army, and the role of the Church. This wasn't all down to Napoleon, of course. It was the work of many people and committees, but it was Napoleon's power and authority that made it possible to get everything into place. After years of indecision, corruption and compromise in French government, this First Consul was actually getting things done.

HEIR STYLE

Napoleon now looked to the future. He didn't think that the ideals of the revolution – liberty, equality and fraternity – and the idea of a monarchy were total opposites. Why couldn't they work together: a revolutionary new government, ruled by a king? When the exiled Louis XVIII wrote to Napoleon suggesting he be put on the throne, Napoleon famously replied that he couldn't expect to be allowed to return to France. 'It would mean marching over 100,000 dead bodies.' (King Louis XVI had, of course, been executed, and Louis XVII had died in prison, which left Louis XVIII.) If not a king for France, then why not an emperor? Why shouldn't Napoleon make himself emperor with a son and heir to take his place when he died? He liked it! The only problem was that he and Josephine had no children of their own . . . Of course, Napoleon could name one of his many brothers as heir, but he didn't seem too chuffed with that idea. Then Josephine's daughter gave birth to a bouncing baby boy, Charles, in October 1802. Now Napoleon could name his step-grandson heir, if he was allowed to. But it was a matter of one thing at a time . . .

CONSULATE FOR LIFE

By April 1802, Napoleon's popularity was at an all-time high, despite the odd assassination attempt, now and then. The new governing body, called the Senate, now proposed that the consulate – with Napoleon as First Consul – rule for another ten years. But Napoleon insisted on a plebiscite (which sounds a bit like a parasite but is, in fact, a direct vote by the electorate). The proposal? To make Napoleon First Consul for life. 8,374 people voted against the idea. 3.6 million voted for it. At least, those are the official figures.

AND NEXT?

Now that, like a monarch, he had the job for as long as he lived, Napoleon wanted to be able to choose his successor, like a monarch, too. He created a new Privy Council and

changed the constitution so that he could name his heir, just as planned. Now all he needed was a more impressive title than 'consul'. He got that when, in May 1804, the Senate announced that – subject to another one of those plebiscites I talked about earlier – his new title would be 'emperor'. Not bad for a little Corsican from a family of eight, huh?

THE EMPEROR NAPOLEON

Napoleon's coronation as 'Emperor of the French' took place in Notre Dame Cathedral on 2 December 1804, where he was crowned by the Pope himself. Napoleon then crowned Josephine, who promptly burst into tears. (That evening, he made her wear her crown at supper!) Many courtiers and palace servants who'd served the dead king now returned to serve the man who was king in everything but name! The revolution had swept away the nobility but now the Emperor Napoleon was creating a whole new layer of hereditary Imperial nobles of his own. He handed out titles, riches and captured territory left, right and centre.

BE AFRAID

Napoleon believed in a hands-on approach to governing. He didn't trust others to get on with it, and he was convinced that the way to hold on to his power was to constantly supervise those under him, and to create fear. He once pointed out that both at home and abroad he reigned only through the fear he inspired. He began getting rid of the bright advisers with ideas and suggestions of their own, replacing them with a bunch of 'yes-men' who never dared argue with a word he said.

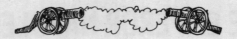

FUNNY HA HA/FUNNY PECULIAR

How much the Emperor had a public persona and a private persona is hard to say. ('Persona' means personality. In fact, it's the word 'personality' with the '-lity' chopped off.) If he wanted to rule by fear, he'd need a fearful public persona, but what was he like behind the scenes? He certainly had a sense of humour. When a lunatic managed to confront him, declaring undying love for Napoleon's wife, Napoleon suggested that the man choose someone else to confide in! When he was served a late-night snack of a cold chicken with parts missing, he asked since when had there been one-legged, one-winged chickens, and pulled the ears of the servant whom, it turned out, had eaten them! (He liked hair-pulling and nose-tweaking too.)

EYES ON ENGLAND

Meanwhile, he hadn't given up on plans to invade England one day – it had become an obsession – and, between 1803 and 1805, preparations had continued, though some people argue that the 'Grand Army' he was supposedly raising and training to fight the British was really being prepared to fight other continental powers. There were, however, definite plans to send 2,000 ships and boats to England, carrying round about 100,000 men to seize London. That was about the same number of troops as was in the entire British army so, had the French turned up, their victory would have been pretty well assured! The only problem was the same problem as always: Lord Nelson and the British fleet.

THE BATTLE OF TRAFALGAR

Emperor Napoleon's plan was to force the British fleet to split up and go to defend various British colonies, leaving England open to attack. After various minor skirmishes came the Battle of Trafalgar. The French fleet, under the command of a man named Villeneuve, left Cadiz (a cape in south-west Spain) – along with Spanish allies – on the orders of the Emperor, and was met by the British under Lord Nelson on 21 October 1805. The combined French and Spanish fleets were humiliatingly defeated in the fighting that followed and the victorious British even managed to capture twenty enemy ships! The one crumb of comfort for Napoleon was that the British hero Lord Nelson was killed in the battle, but there would be others who could take his place. Napoleon now abandoned all immediate thoughts of invading England.

IT'S NOT FAIR! THIS 'GET A LIFE' BOOK SHOULD HAVE BEEN ABOUT ME

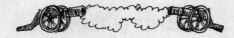

THE CONTINENTAL SYSTEM

Unable to defeat the British fleet fair and square, Napoleon decided on a more subtle approach. If he could bankrupt Britain, then the British wouldn't have the money to maintain and support such a fine fleet. And how could he achieve this? By introducing a 'continental system of exclusion'. In other words, if Napoleon could stop Britain selling its goods to any parts of continental Europe under French control (which was much of it), Britain would soon be in a right financial pickle . . . and the more countries Napoleon invaded, the fewer countries Britain could trade with!

WIVES AND HEIRS

The problem of not having an heir closer than a step-grandson still plagued Napoleon. It was obvious that Josephine could not give him the children he so desperately needed in order to continue the Bonaparte dynasty. Finally, despite the fact that he still loved her, he decided he must divorce her. (She had a screaming fit on the carpet but, after that, took it very well.) In 1808, there had been plans for Napoleon to marry the Tsar of Russia's sister, Catherine, but this came to nothing. In 1810, he married a nineteen-year-old Austrian archduchess called Marie Louise. Marie Louise was the niece of Marie Antoinette, who'd been King Louis XVI's queen and executed along with him. After the marriage, Napoleon took to referring to the dead king as 'my uncle'! A year later, Marie Louise gave birth to a son. Napoleon was ecstatic, the people of Paris celebrated, and the boy was given the title 'King of Rome'! I should point out here that, as well as a new wife and a legitimate son and heir, Napoleon already had a mistress (girlfriend) called Marie Walewska and two illegitimate sons. ('Illegitimate' means being born outside marriage. Illegitimate children didn't have the rights of children born to married parents.) The first boy grew up to be a French Foreign Minister.

VICTORY AFTER VICTORY

It's important not to lose sight of the fact that Napoleon was still a great soldier, which is why he was so popular in France. One of the greatest. In the Napoleonic Wars – named after guess who – he virtually ruled the entire continent of Europe, after the Treaty of Tilsit. He defeated the Austrians at Austerlitz in 1805 (possibly the greatest military victory in his life), the Prussians at Jena in 1806 and the Russians at Friedland in 1807 (which means he didn't even get to take a year off in between). It was only during the Peninsular campaign in Spain that things began to go horribly wrong for him. Napoleon later wrote: 'The Spanish ulcer destroyed me.'

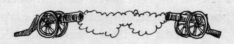

KEEP IT IN THE FAMILY

Always loyal to old friends, Napoleon heaped titles and honours on members of his family. With the French Empire stretched across Europe, he now had many important titles to give away. He offered to make his brother Lucien King of Spain, but Lucien refused. Napoleon didn't like Lucien's wife and thought he should marry someone else. Lucien chose to stay married to the one he loved and to live (in retirement) in Italy. So Napoleon made his

elder brother, Joseph – whom he'd already made King of Naples – King of Spain instead. Brothers Louis and Jérôme were made Kings of Holland and Westphalia respectively. (Westphalia was a state in Prussia, now in Germany). His sister Caroline was Grand Duchess of Berg and, later, Queen of Naples, and Elisa was made Grand Duchess of Tuscany.

THE NAPOLEONIC CODE

Whenever France gained new territory, the Napoleonic Code was introduced there so, pretty much wherever you were in the vast French empire, you were governed by the same laws. The Napoleonic Code contained Napoleon's version of the main principles of the French Revolution: liberty, equality (of sorts) and a fair, open court system for all to see, with juries. He believed that, if the Code was applied everywhere, it would be easier for the French to keep her – countries are often 'shes' for some reason – territories bound together as one.

NO, OF COURSE THAT'S NOT THE NAPOLEONIC CODE! THAT'S ANCIENT EGYPTIAN HIEROGLYPHS!!!

THE PENINSULAR WAR

Napoleon invaded Portugal in 1807 and it was a year later that he placed Joseph on the Spanish throne. Revolts in Spain followed. The British then intervened in Portugal, defeating the French forces at Vimeiro. The man in charge in Portugal was called Sir Arthur Wellesley and became one of the most famous soldiers ever, ever, ever. If you're wondering why you've never heard of him, then I should point out that he later became the Duke of Wellington. More familiar now, huh? It was as Sir Arthur, though, that he invaded Spain and routed – a fabulous word, which means 'defeated and caused to flee', and almost as good as 'pillage' – the French forces at Vitoria in 1813. (He wasn't made Duke of Wellington until 1814.)

THOSE TROUBLESOME RUSKIES

In 1811, Napoleon decided to have one big – hopefully final – battle against the Russians, having learnt that they were thinking of attacking French forces in Germany. One of his biggest problems, though, was that his troops would be fighting on two fronts at once. Whilst he was massing his troops in Poland ready to invade Russia, he already had thousands of troops fighting in Spain. (Some historians think that Napoleon might have gone a bit bananas!) Despite this, Napoleon still managed to raise an army of about 600,000 men.

PLEASE STOP AND FIGHT!

In June 1812, Napoleon crossed into Russia with 450,000 of his troops. (The remaining 150,000 would follow.) He hoped for one big battle and to get it over and done with but, having only 160,000 troops, the Russians knew that they were hugely outnumbered and that it would be crazy to fight. They did the only sensible thing they could: retreat (which is military-speak for 'ran away'). Napoleon's troops kept on after them, hoping they might stop and fight. On 17 August, Napoleon bombarded the city of Smolensk, which the Russian forces abandoned two days later, breaking through the French advance party and continuing their flight to Moscow.

SHRINKING FORCES

Napoleon was getting fed up. He'd wanted a glorious victory and Russia under his control by now. Instead, he had the task of keeping 450,000 men on the move, fed and healthy! As it was, by the time he faced the Russian forces on the banks of the river Moskova, he only had 130,000 men fighting fit. In the two months since the invasion began, thousands had been lost through sickness or by deserting. This is what generals call 'wastage'! In the fighting on 7 September, the French casualties were about 30,000, but the Russians lost 58,000 and retreated further still.

INTO MOSCOW

Napoleon and his forces entered Moscow on 14 September 1812. He found the place deserted! That night, fires blazed away in the city and lasted for five whole days. At first, Napoleon thought that they'd been started by his own drunken troops but, when he found that every fire-pump and fire engine in the city was missing, it dawned on him that this was a part of a cunning Russian plan. Napoleon hung around, grumpily, for a month in the Moscow palace of the Kremlin, sending messages to the Tsar in St Petersburg, but Alexander didn't bother to reply!

FROM BAD TO DREADFUL

On 19 October 1812, Napoleon left Moscow with his army of 100,000 – you didn't forget the 30,000 casualties, did you? – and decided that they should spend the bitter winter in Smolensk. They reached there on 3 November. The first snow didn't fall until six days later, but his army was already dying of hunger, not cold. When they finally left Smolensk, only 40,000 troops were fighting fit . . . After skirmishes at Krasnoe, Minsk, and Vilna – when the harshest of harsh winters had done its worst – Napoleon left what little remained of his army on 6 December, to hurry back to Paris. News of the terrible bungling in Russia had led to the rumour that the Emperor Napoleon was actually dead, so he wanted to show his face. Of the 600,000 troops who'd taken part in the attempted invasion of Russia, only 30,000 survived.

THE BATTLE OF THE NATIONS

So Napoleon still had to face the Russians, British, Prussians and Austrians another time. After various military campaigns, everything came to a head at the Battle of the Nations outside the German city of Leipzig on the 16, 17 and 18 October 1813. Napoleon was doomed. He had

just 160,000 men whilst the enemy allied forces numbered about 320,000. Not only that, his allies, the Bavarians, promptly switched sides to the enemy! During the French retreat into Leipzig, a bridge over the river Elster was blown up before planned, trapping thousands of French troops on the wrong side. Napoleon returned home defeated, with less than 60,000 men.

A REFUSAL TO QUIT

The humiliating defeat at the Battle of the Nations meant that France's empire now lay in ruins. Holland then rose up against its French masters, and the victorious allies declared that they would attack France unless, of course, Napoleon agreed to peace terms. The British were eager to see a king back on the throne of France, with the country returned to its pre-revolution size and borders. In February 1814, these terms were put before Napoleon. He refused, preferring to try his chances against an allied attack, then negotiating more preferable terms.

THE BEGINNING OF THE END

His generals were war-weary and his regular troops young and ill-trained, but Napoleon had great plans. Paris would be the enemy allies' obvious target. Rather than defending the city from within, Napoleon's forces would attack the advancing army from the side and the rear. This might just have worked if it wasn't for the state of Imperial France. The regime – his government – was falling apart around him. Some wanted to push for peace with the allies. Some simply wanted to overthrow Napoleon. Some wanted nothing to do with anything. The country had lost her heart.

LET BATTLE COMMENCE

When the allies finally invaded with an army of 300,000 in 1814, Napoleon could only raise an army of about 120,000 men. Despite this, Napoleon had his first victory at Brienne, on 29 January. (Those of you with brains the size of planets will recall that Brienne was where the young Napoleon went to military academy. The rest of us will simply have to marvel at your amazing memories.) He suffered a defeat three days later at La Rothiére, which is probably what made the allies overconfident. On 10 and 11 February, at Champaubert and Montmirail, he caused the allies heavy casualties and even managed to send plenty of Russian prisoners to Paris to be paraded in the streets as a morale-booster for the French people.

YET MORE VICTORIES

Despite the odds, Napoleon still had more victories in him. On 18 February, he won the battle of Montereau and the allies' overconfidence was now replaced with feelings of disbelief, doom and gloom. Napoleon tried to divide the enemy by offering to negotiate a separate peace with Austria, but the British got the allies to sign an agreement that none of them would negotiate separately and that, if needs be, the war against France would go on for another twenty years.

THE MONARCHY RETURNS

A number of battles followed with no clear victors, but when news reached the allies that morale was at an all-time low in Paris, they decided that they might as well ignore

Napoleon's army and march on the Parisians. By the time Tsar Alexander and his forces reached the capital city, a Frenchman called Talleyrand was in charge there. When the allies issued a statement saying that they no longer recognized Napoleon as ruler of France and that the defeated French should rule up a new constitution, it was Talleyrand who formed a provisional government. On 6 April 1814, its members voted that Louis XVIII be crowned king. The monarchy was back.

END OF AN ERA

On 12 April, Napoleon tried to kill himself in the near-empty palace of Fontainebleau. He took poison, he later said, because he didn't want his face to be messed up by a pistol shot if his body was to lie in state! A better explanation as to why he had to resort to poison, as a means of trying to kill himself, was probably because his servant had emptied all his pistols! Fortunately – or unfortunately – for Napoleon, the poison had been knocking about for years and was useless. He lived. The Treaty of Fontainebleau was enforced. Napoleon Bonaparte was no longer Emperor of France.

MEETING HIS WATERLOO

Napoleon was met at Fontainebleau by the British, Austrian, Russian and Prussian Commissioners. On 20 April, they left the palace and began their journey to Elba, the island west of Italy that was to be the exiled ex-emperor's new home. He hadn't seen his wife or son for ages, and missed them terribly. He received a mixed reception when passing through towns and villages. In some places there were cries of 'Long live the Emperor!' Elsewhere he was booed. Once he even passed an effigy of himself being burned by an angry mob! He was then put on board the British ship the *Undaunted* and arrived at the island of Elba on 4 May.

NOT ALONE

If you imagine Napoleon's time in exile on the island of Elba must have been similar to being shipwrecked on a desert island, you couldn't be more wrong. Apart from Bertrand, Napoleon's Grand Marshal of the Palace at Fontainebleau, and various servants, 700 of his Old Guard arrived from France (three hundred more men than agreed in the treaty, but who was counting)! He also had plenty of visitors, including his mother, sister Pauline and even his mistress Marie Walewska. He was even allowed to 'rule' his new mini-kingdom.

BIDING HIS TIME

Meanwhile, all was not well back in France which had been so kindly restored to its old pre-revolution self by the allies, then left to its own devices. Louis XVIII himself was unpopular and rumour was rife. People feared that the Church and old nobility might regain their original stranglehold on the country, seizing back their old lands. And the army still had a soft spot for Napoleon, more famous for his victories than his defeats. The French king chose to ignore those parts of the Treaty of Fontainebleau that he didn't like, so declared that he wouldn't be paying the exiled Napoleon the 'pension' promised to him.

TIME TO ACT

On 26 February 1815, Napoleon sneaked away from Elba – under the noses of the British, who turned up two days later – in the battleship *Inconstant*. He made it to France, landing near Antibes on 28 February or 1 March (depending on who you believe). From there, with a band of less than 1,000 loyal men he headed for Paris. Like any good soldier, he hadn't acted without 'intelligence' (advance information), and felt pretty sure that they'd reach the capital 'without firing a shot'. Near Grenoble, a battalion of royalist soldiers blocked the road. Napoleon ordered his men to put their muskets under their arms out of harm's way. He then faced the battalion. 'Kill your emperor if you wish,' he shouted. Ignoring their commander's orders to fire, the battalion surrounded him, cheering 'Long live the Emperor!' Then the whole garrison town of Grenoble joined him!

INTO PARIS INTO POWER

Although one of the King's marshals famously promised to bring Napoleon back to Paris in an iron cage, on 20 March, Napoleon was carried up the steps of the palace not by his enemies but by wildly cheering supporters. Louis XVIII had wisely fled the day before. Now Napoleon decided that his best chance of staying popular with the people was to have a good battle – after all, that's what he was known to be good at! He knew that his enemy allies were fed up with fighting and, if he could have a few swift victories, he might be able to agree a peace deal where they accepted him as boss of France.

BACK IN THE THICK OF IT

In June 1815, he raised an army of 250,000 troops, made up of a mixture of professional soldiers and civilian Frenchmen called up to fight. 120,000 were ready to attack at any time. The only enemy forces near France were on the Belgian frontier. The 210,000 or so allied troops were divided into 120,000 Prussians under the command of a man called Blücher, and 90,000 British, Belgian, Dutch and Hanoverian troops under the command of – dramatic drum roll – Wellington. Napoleon's army attacked Blücher's before they really knew what was happening and Wellington's troops were slow in coming to their defence. It would probably have been a great French victory if Napoleon's general Ney hadn't been so slow to act. Napoleon was still victorious, but he hadn't destroyed the Prussians as he'd hoped.

FATAL FLAWS

On 17 June 1815, Napoleon ordered 33,000 of his troops to find the retreating Prussians while he and Ney faced Wellington with the remaining troops. He assumed that Blücher had taken his Prussian troops east, when they'd actually gone north and were heading for Wellington. When Napoleon's force of 74,000 men faced Wellington's 67,000 at Mont St Jean on 18 June, therefore, he had no idea that the Prussian support forces were on their way.

THE FIELD OF BATTLE

Because Wellington was there before Napoleon, he got to choose the battlefield for the Battle of Waterloo, and the position of his troops on it. His men stood with a slight hill behind them – a hill behind which Wellington's reserve troops could gather, safe from cannon fire. After a day of rain, the place was muddy to say the least. To say that Napoleon underestimated Wellington would be a bit like saying elephants are slightly bigger than fleas. He said that Wellington was a bad general, that the English were bad troops and that the battle would be 'a picnic'. Napoleon only bothered to work out the general plan of attack, but decided to leave the actual carrying out of the plan and tactical manoeuvres to Ney.

THE BATTLE OF WATERLOO

The main French attack began at 1.30 p.m. and things soon went wrong. Not only did Wellington's forces repel them, with heavy casualties, but columns of Prussian soldiers were now approaching their right flank. As if that wasn't bad enough, Napoleon now learnt that his reinforcements were being held up by another bunch of Prussians about thirteen miles away! Rather than retreating, Napoleon now decided that the battle must be won before the Prussians turned up in force. He sent 10,000 troops to try to hold off the approaching Prussians then ordered Ney to lead another attack on the English at 3.30 p.m. This Ney did but, at first, he only sent in the cavalry (men on horses) instead of the infantry (foot soldiers) too. At 6.30 p.m. – everything seems to have happened at half-past-something – the French infantry managed to drive through English lines, making gaps. For some unexplained reason, Napoleon refused to send in the French reserves to widen the gaps until 7.00 p.m., by which time, Wellington had closed ranks. Wellington's cavalry then charged and the French fled. Only 8,000 or so escaped alive and unharmed. Napoleon was not the great military man he used to be. The Battle of Waterloo was lost.

PARISIAN PROBLEMS

Back in Paris, things didn't turn out too well for Napoleon either. On 22 June, he abdicated yet again. He abdicated in favour of his son declaring the toddler to be Emperor Napoleon II, but the provisional government decided to ask Louis XVIII back instead. So, on 8 July, the King turned up in Paris once again, after being away for exactly 100 days!

INTO EXILE ONCE MORE

The new French government, eager to get their ex-emperor out of the way, asked the British – with their dominant navy – to allow Napoleon safe passage to the USA. The British refused, and Napoleon gave himself up to Captain Maitland of the British ship the *Bellerophon*. (Bellerophon was a Greek hero who'd got too big for his boots and tried to claim his place amongst the gods. He ended up falling to earth with a nasty bump. Seem familiar?) When the ship docked at the English ports of Torbay and Plymouth, loads of sightseers turned up in boats, trying to catch a glimpse of the great man!

DOWNGRADED AND DEGRADED

When aboard the *Bellerophon*, Napoleon had been treated like an emperor, with great respect. He hoped that he might be allowed to settle in Britain – even writing to the Prince Regent – so was horrified when he learnt that he was to be sent to the island of St Helena in the South Atlantic. He was even more upset when he found out that he wasn't going to

BEFORE WE START, DO YOU MIND IF I GET RID OF ALL THE KINGS?

be treated like an ex-emperor there, but as an ordinary retired general on a pension! He and his entourage were transferred to the *Northumberland* and the three-month journey to St Helena began. He spent much of his time dictating his memoirs and, in the evenings, playing cards with the English naval officers.

HIS FINAL DAYS

Napoleon spent the last six years of his life on St Helena. He started off living in a pavilion in someone else's garden whilst his house was being prepared! When he moved into his new home, a new English governor arrived on the island: Sir Hudson Lowe. The two men hated each other from the word go. In 1818, Napoleon became ill and, by 1819, was in great pain and unable to eat. He died on 5 May 1821. His very last word was 'Josephine'. Lowe thought Napoleon had been faking! At the time, the French thought Napoleon had died of liver disease. The British thought it was stomach cancer. Later, two new theories emerged. The first was that it was simply an ulcer which, if treated properly, could have been cured. The second theory is far more strange.

KILLER WALLPAPER

The wallpaper in Napoleon's rooms was a beautiful green. In those days, the poison arsenic was often used as a green colouring (in things that weren't to be drunk or eaten, of course). There is a theory that the damp climate caused the paper to give off arsenic fumes that Napoleon breathed in day in and day out and which, therefore, eventually poisoned and killed him. If you think that's unlikely, there's a twist to the theory: that the wallpaper was *deliberately* impregnated with extra arsenic with the express purpose of murdering Napoleon. The house was especially decorated for Napoleon by the British before he moved in, remember. Was it some dastardly British plot? Perhaps we'll never know.

WHAT NEXT?

Napoleon's son died aged twenty-one, by which time he was no longer 'King of Rome' but the Duke of Reichstadt in Austria. The Bonaparte family did, however, get to rule France once more. Napoleon's nephew Louis – son of his own brother Louis – became Emperor Napoleon III, when France became an imperial nation again in 1852. (Napoleon was his second name.) Napoleon himself, or at least his body, had already been returned to France in 1840, where it was buried with great ceremony.

THE LEGEND

Napoleon once said that 'a man is only a man', but the legend of Napoleon lives on. There are few men and women in history who are immediately identifiable by one name alone – Caesar, Ghandi, Churchill, for example – but even fewer who are identifiable simply by their first name alone. Napoleon is one of a rare breed, and he certainly earned his place amongst them. Standing just 158cm tall he was, in many ways, a giant.

TIMELINE,
at home and abroad

1769   Napoleon is born on the island of Corsica
1775   *David Bushnell builds a submarine*
1789   The French Revolution
1796   Napoleon marries Josephine
1779   The Brumaire *coup d'ètat*
        Napoleon becomes First Consul
1802   Napoleon voted ruler for life
1804   Napoleon named 'Emperor of the French'
1805   French fleet defeated by Nelson at the Battle of
        Trafalgar
1808   Napoleon divorces Josephine
1810   Napoleon marries Marie Louise
1812   Napoleon enters Moscow
1813   *Jane Austin's novel* Pride and Prejudice *is
        published*
1814   Napoleon abdicates
        Louis XVIII crowned King of France
        Napoleon exiled on Elba
        George Stephenson builds his first steam train
1815   Napoleon returns to power in France
        Loses Battle of Waterloo against Wellington's
        forces
        Exiled to St Helena
1819   *Queen Victoria is born*
1821   Napoleon dies